Gallery Books
Editor: Peter Fallon

HAD I A THOUSAND LIVES

Medbh McGuckian

HAD I A THOUSAND LIVES

Gallery Books

Had I a Thousand Lives
is first published
simultaneously in paperback
and in a clothbound edition
on 17 July 2003.

The Gallery Press
Loughcrew
Oldcastle
County Meath
Ireland

ISBN 1 85235 346 5 (*paperback*)
       1 85235 347 3 (*clothbound*)

A CIP catalogue record for this book
is available from the British Library.

The Gallery Press acknowledges the financial assistance
of An Chomhairle Ealaíon / The Arts Council, Ireland.

Contents

for Clemency Emmet,
with gratitude

By my conduct I do not consider that I have incurred any moral guilt. I have committed no moral evil. I do not want the many and bright examples of those who have gone before me, but did I want this encouragement the recent example of a youthful hero, a martyr in the cause of liberty, who had just died for his country, would inspire me . . . He was surrounded by everything which could endear the world to him, in the bloom of youth, with fond attachments, and with all the fascinating charms of youth and innocence. To his death I look back, even in this state, with rapture.

I have travelled much and seen various parts of the world, and I think the Irish the most virtuous nation on the face of the earth — they are a good and brave people, and had I a thousand lives, I would yield them in their service.

— Thomas Russell
October 1803

It is well, therefore, that we should examine and find out why Ireland has placed him foremost among her saints of nationality; why she honors him most of all those who have laid down their lives to serve her. The Catholic Church has a curious ceremony which precedes the canonization of a saint. One states all that can be said against him and then another refutes these accusations. The saint's life is carefully examined, and so I would have you examine with me the life of Emmet.

— W B Yeats
New York, 1904

River of January

I do not sing of arms and the man,
I have nothing to say which I can say.
People walk about as if they own
where they are, and they do.

But those separated by a forest
of error from the separated
call the deadly loneliness
by many other names.

How and why do we dream
of living in unity
with the island that has become
as the forest was, warming our hands

in her warm breast? Creating
a flower-rich shelter, or the heart
of a nest, in a wood left untouched
by the prospering suggestion of orchards?

It is just a promise and strong
but beautiful like every promise
in its pure mountain form
whose shadow was the forest cleared.

The old meanings of the forest
read the seasons in the seasonless,
treeless, herbless, overfished
sea bespread with eye-driven ships

and the fixed salts of plants
in the sand which paves the sea.
They fall into a light-bringing
language, till all the light

within the light, deceptive
as the leaf fall of the day
from a tree that has died in sleep,
satisfies, by its quality of chaliceness.

Slieve Gallion

for Emily

That great central bone of mountain
belittling the apple-shaped earth,
or the unhandled marble of its head-bone,
warmed me to the very eyelids.

Find-spots of Judas-coloured blossom
wove bird-lure and man-burning furnaces
on its high quarried joy —
in a place not to be trodden

the neck-fetters of an asphalt smooth,
regrettably modern road paved the thread
of its voice — its breath-poem
into battle letters, its mouth music

into a pocketful of women-nation-
voters. I looked fifteen times
for that monosexual, banished river
smell, for its unnailing.

Nightingale-nights

No one was at the pier
but the all-severing wave,
that by-play,
those plunges;
the softened white of the moon
was in other places.

I had meant to talk endlessly
with him, and come near him
in words, a little way
up the side of the cup, to
there where we first
talked of war.

My brotherly fears meant
stepping out alone into company,
and expecting to remain alone,
or far off sideways,
between barely and not quite standing,
set asunder by the asides of talk.

If he was there, living,
after a week of the same grim giving,
he could not help but be
the one thing he had denied himself
the right to be — the greatest space
blooming without aim,

a hill-mass which would hold
the snow in big, free hauls,
banished from its kingdom
but facing towards it,
its villages in view
to his eyes of seafarer's blue,

eyes that after a winged glance
reflect the sea or a shell's
embrace. If I could see him
before with his eyes he asked
me not to ask, I can't think
what he would ask

my forgiveness for,
such days as do not belong to death,
or to its deathly morning,
the yearly infusions from his rare
and recent hands whose lines
represent transparency:

the precious still-life
and rich dream-supper,
growing far out of life from within,
of the tones of his voice
fastened to a page
in only apparently unanswered letters.

And when I slumbered
with the parklike common
of his poems on my breast,
I never measured the pang there
that makes poetry,
losing a part of my eternity,

seeing the broad completed shelf
of his books like incised
sunflowers on a wooden balcony —
the outer man, his garments
hung up in a row
with nobody inside.

The Rock Dove

A source of air like a couched lance,
a colour that makes me think of France:
trees swinging open in all directions,
the land beginning to grow again
in the low-angled, soft yellow sunlight.

The posted soldiers that had fighting cocks
strapped to their saddles now allow us
to try on their hats, rolling up their bedding.
The river wide and slow at its mouth
has a heavy, sickly smell from all the blood.

A woman is seen laying salt
in the doorway of a woman of another rhythm.
In the rosemary hedge where a nightingale
has speared himself on a thorn,
it's like black wine, cloaked in its own feathers and skin.

Petit Bleu

We need a verb meaning either
to send someone to paradise
or to keep a hawk from sleep
in order to tame it.

I only have to look up
to see the mounted policeman
at lamp-post level, opposite my window,
the great boots and pointed helmets
drilling outside autumn,

while the local policeman
has nothing to do, and is sad,
as the military band plays
its hundredth *Carmen*,

like very old, old men
who have four days to play
with, whose funerals
I miss like your smooth eyes . . .

Because of your picturesque
ideas and past, you sprinkle
small pieces of torn letters
around the green yard
of a luxury prison,

flashes of summer
through your one November,
pieces of winter
through your summer hospital;

and whenever the letter *R*
crops up, it can be seen
to refer to other *R*s,
or the eternal letter *L*.

You burn like an extra-
special sunset
in the warmth of your bed,
the very soul of the prison,

the throbbing streets
of your every pore
tingling with liberty
in the immutability
of your 'bedroom'.

As yet I've kissed
nothing of yours but jewellery
of no value, the palest pencil
arriving as a madness,
an indelible moonburn
harvested at one in the morning . . .

On the north side
where no one walks
except in new shoes returning
from Mass, the shop-fronts are painted
sang-de-boeuf, the old roofs
take a one-in-ten climb
between red walls.

The ground-colour changes
on the day after rain

like childish breasts scored
by the introduction of gold,
but safe at last
from the too brilliant stars.

And at eight sharp by the palace
clock, all the doomed in all but name,
born in the sea-port
of this famous island

out of the yellow election posters
of this 'cimetière marin',
become as strange as the sky
over so many years of slow
hours of sea, the half-breath
way . . . lace falls.

A Religion of Writing

The island's lock weakened
as in dreams; the sea-beauty
of the air was moved
by warmed music which caused
that question to vanish.

Dreams as common as rain
returning to the outdoors
one whom the earth has reclaimed
in the passage from the name
to the body, the remoteness
of name to meaning.

Despite the thicket, the writing
is set low, half-empty lines
with ivy leaves and fruits
acting as punctuation.
Such unsteady capitals,

the backward *S*, the *L*
with its foot slanting sharply
downwards, the *B* with detached
loops, a *G* consisting of two opposing
curves, a *Q* with its extended tail

taken up inside, a long palm-like
Y. There are cuts reinforcing
the heads and the forking
of the uprights, letters of smaller
size placed inside others.

Winged death with two conversing
skeletons, a flame
with no clothing,
a death's head carved
with a human head inside it.

Blue Kasina

1

You walk as if you are kissing the earth
(she is breathing — why not me?)
or tapping a page like a drum, you invite
the bell of my hardly used breasts to sound.

My second breast imbibes your graces,
the mind-river of my very first love,
which lets the leaves pass through
as when he wanted my face to be more stricken.

You march your breastless body
back and forth with all its volumes
like a frontier, still agitated
by piety, blood beneath your everyday verdure:

as the semi-divine womb is able
to move around in search of moisture,
and will find it in an opening between two arms,
a path slit as if for letters.

2

I am sight-singing you, music
made out of music, listening to the unfamiliar
Mass of your male womb and robust hymen,
your someoneness, paid not to undress.

I am just this much inside your breath
all by itself where you die into
the tide of each unique breath
as the full language watering your mouth

with flow lines of water, their colourlessness
almost intense. The drop of my dress
into the pool of my dress is a brown garland,
a fresh crown, that has never been so closed before.

And for seventeen minutes I brighten
by watching like rarely observable
star sets how your thoughts end,
greeting your rust in whatever rings and shines.

3

The glassed subconcious of the city
is overwhelmingly sweetened, the narrowness
of the light is false, the shadows false,
draping the window-cushions with gold watches.

So now each soldier has swallowed a draught
of *eau-de-vie* in which the flag's
ashes have been dissolved, we can
begin again with the *A* names

in the wood-book, using the soot of wood.
It is a kind of confusion of faithfulness,
this unkind holding of the torch of wishlessness,
that turns gently within my unmet gaze

an after-key not turned far enough
to snag and soften all about it
the regrowth on the cleared table
whose threading would give mile by mile.

Hearing the Weather Fall

The shutters folded back in their frames
with a pale movement,
a pacific repetition,
and only mirrors followed
to pierce where the day was stored,

each so enisled
and smiled at
by the sympathy of the tides,
looking less arrived
in a waveless bay,
and over, a bay of fields . . .

Now crowningly,
the droop of the sky
into my morning —
somebody would pay
for the night, a very soon
weekend — for the braking,
for the slowing-up,

for the uncharted pain
as then still forgiven.
A never-fighter,
running out a hand
to ask as from a death-bed
why this loves to happen,

I'd rather this fishing village
at the end of the world,
lying down and down a dull sea,
than the bound slope
of a suburban hill,
or everywhere that one visits
acquisitively,

than library voices
in the changed room.
The country's essence,
moored at the north
but with an air of being
washed out west,

could not forgo that kindling,
the arm which tightened
like a steady look from his
long eyes, knowing
the wrong wings are crossed up there.

The Chimney Boys

It is late earlier. The faded biscuit-pink
of the infill building inflames the edge
of the slanted blue and white chessboard.

Those darling policemen, we thought,
but no, they really were insurgents,
a swatch or crumbs of colour going dark.

Every room has a soul if it can be prised
open, a little shy of its own beauty,
under the feudal right of introspecting houses.

But those who saw them skylarking
in the gutters, looking clean and wholesome,
were unable to find any text to discredit it.

Factory children, valued as little as rabbits,
or decaying birds transfixed on a dog-spear,
small gentry, urchins in dreary gambols,

they were climbing boys, boys of the best size,
little boys for soot-caked flues,
seeds of sleep harvesting the dew

on what was left of Saturday, for an ideal
Sabbath. A pewful of children throbbing
for liberty, a bundle of jointed sticks,

lashed from their beds clutching their clothes
over their arms by loving Sabbatarian
engines purifying their manhood.

A boy is hard to quench, mingled
too much with bitter wood; but what is a toasted
child, lying in his nigritude,

his corkscrew motion, his sable consolation,
to a deranged dinner party? Murder by proxy,
a melancholy but imperious necessity.

Four assorted clergy, bigot and crank,
with scriptural thrust and parry ready
to add their own enemies to theirs,

pin the bosoms of their lute-string shirts
back, as if they had saved as many
lives as Marconi, normal persons,

six-pounders spraying glass marbles
and clay balls. Soon there would be brooches
for sale with 'God over, curse Great Britain'.

Then the vulture, emblem of time,
calling the hour by another name,
will lay sunflowers at their feet on the longest day.

The Surrender Dance

Some snowdrops in an envelope
had slipped out of heaven
like an angel's life.

I fell in love with a sunflower
as my window to my father
not conceived in colour.

Some old prayers were answered
to my sweet kneeling, which I say
happened before roads were marked

or the Rêve d'Or roses put
all the left-hand corner
into over-cultivated shadow.

The storm of rice and slippers
was as odd a lullaby
as full voices and guitar music:

we woke to the *Pax Brittanica*
with a widowed sense of a world
ending in a psalm.

Asking for the Alphabet Back

1

She could not even remember the word
for water. A single drop
in a grey wave lied to her,
singing the news that clawed and stung.

The un-men were not only men
but her men. They brimmed over
the symmetrical watchtowers, the wall spoke
as though it were the unbroken Host.

2

A blend of new forest with a pure stand
of high forest, the year agreed
into the evening's understory of holly,
from the cratered ground renamed
for the month in which they captured her.

Each lighter month anchors a little more
of the next; and the praying towns' triduum
prayed the bullet through her heart
as English followed the roads, its tidings'
malady amputating the wildscape.

But some member of the lily family
had worn a garment in the dancing
which filled it bullet-proof —
a ghost-shirt left by a god for a man,
its bright English keeping the dark alive.

Bedroom with Chrysanthemums

I like the wordlessness of countries changing
into the next, of being spilt from one world
to its brother, where sky may become weather.

It takes the strain off my lips, their loving
each other, being rubbed smooth and jerked out
into talk that smears a ring around my mind
like winter's soot on my blotting-paper wallpaper.

My desk floods till the window ripples, breaks
the flowering image of the garden. The fluent morning
with a red breadth to it from some sunset
skims the tops of words as one calm jewel,
and ends abruptly after pouring one cup.

I meant the outer story in its second meaning,
I meant the actual voice gone
into the position of the one asked,
my rose-buying old year's walk
that changes name much as it changes direction,
avoiding, by a bedroom way, the chrysanthemums.

Reading in a Library

You wake me up with the name
I carry inside me like a first
language. It becomes needles
on your lips, slightly grey, a waste
of light I swallow like a syrup.

A tree forks at the level
of your eyes, it spreads my dark
dipthong upward like a cup,
I place myself expectantly
under your open hand.

You talk with your hands
like two people, you zigzag
softly from person to person,
rubbing my names together
as if that were your goal,

not pushing my thoughts into
the space beneath the bed.
I bring a sentence to your body,
brimming like an island, I sit
filled with that, as with a bible.

Cathal's Voice

All manner of flavoured chimes
spread my hips boatwise. A people's climate
threaded and sun-toughened
my ruby-echoed bathroom.

My native silence reeled
silently out of reach,
corpses of lupins grassed over
the upside-down stare of the canal,

endlessly circling together
their corkscrewing petals
like great experts in resurrection.
Our voices were surely sleeping

far above us, with elbows poised
high, where the flat air loses
all body. All the rich juices
of the first official language

bulged in the woody sequence of plants
along the hedge, where leaf
was at home with delicate-tongued
leaf. It took the feeble shape

of battlements around my lilac neck,
or a Hesitation valse through numb
furniture, the late-returning traffic
of that completely bilingual, attempted embrace.

The Mirror Game

The voice does not work without time.
— Leonardo da Vinci

It is the moment just before you make the sound.
There is a bottled feeling, as if it fills you,
rising through your whole length to your locked
throat tensions and your rounded lips.

You make the most space possible in your mouth,
tightening the supple organ of your tongue,
and the muscles hidden in your unpeaceful neck,
though your anchored ribs are left free to move.

I have some sense of where the sound begins
in the untense channels of my own unprepared
body, and will lock it in my chest
like a slight warmth on the finger.

Already, when you merely breathe,
the withheld quality of your voice feels
full of voice, as if there is an aura of voice
around you, keeping the voice there.

When you lift the starting-note
and turn it into a spoken word
your voice seems lifeless, absorbed by carpets,
or doesn't sound as if it belongs

to your whole body: it is as if you are sighing.
You blow out a bullet of air,
the lower notes of your breathstream
locking the voice and the word from note to note,

a note, then a higher note,
speaking from each new note
in light, deft movements,
blowing the floor clean.

Some over-musical distortion
in the middle of your voice
flows like an autumn to winter season
through your singer's passage.

I think of the theatre as you
and imagine you to be very light
with a brightness working right through
your continued lightness.

Now is the time for you to play with the sound,
the poems of the world tugging at your throat,
and suddenly it becomes difficult to say
what my meaning feels like

in my poor-sounding tongue-string
barely attached to meaning,
testing for an escape of air;
while the ring and bright overtone

and free sound of your airspill
robs me as a speaker;
for you are living differently,
as you join sound to sound,

inviting me to make the journey
to inhabit you, to let my body change,
or let it work through into voice,
to find your voice and let my body follow.

Lie close, take one sound at a time,
allow the far from conversational sounds
to sink, and make the half-private world
as true for me as possible.

There is no longer an image, only you,
the fluency of a real life.
I try to feel what your tongue and lips
have to do, the straight substitution

of one sound for another,
the consonants which are not used
unless like some strange behaviours
dredged up in sounds which shouldn't be there.

Until I am sure of the new sound,
which is not something you do to,
but something you do with,
and is what its name suggests.

A foot from your mouth, selective as your ear,
I pause to free myself from the forced
croaking of my foreign speech,
as if I choked on a moustache,

or only stammered when it rained;
and try saying a phrase or sentence
forgetting to speak with my man's voice.
Then, partly in a non-speaking journey

to meet me, you walk towards my heavy drapes
till I recognise the road as the laying down
of a voice-track to a picture,
your voice-shape as a night-cool bell.

Anything more we do should be the singing
of a round such as 'Rose, Rose' or 'London's Burning' —
all those honest and usable Englishings
that were the heat-death on lips, pound by pound.

Photograph of a Passerine in Song

His roosting songfulness —
the whisper of his wing music —
I am songless at his far-carrying
flight song.

Rose-breasted, large-eyed,
he gives a call not heard
at any other time,
beginning with a single, begging note,

a subsong of about seven notes,
then turns away his head,
holding up his beak a day's length
to clouds at different levels in the foliage.

Porzana Porzana

The sand-grouse crashes noisily
out of deep rock-cover,
exploding out of his cave's unlined nest
to fly strongly to the wood-edge,

his wing-strokes ending low and
far back. A successful bird
and unmistakable, he can walk
under water or on growing-points

of branches, his habitat when not
at his breeding place the garden
burdened with all manner of grasses
beginning to be mortal.

A good flight-mark is the rusty
crescent on his vinous breast,
feral parure dissolving
in the fraction of a second

like a lesson learnt by heart
but not understood . . .
Through eye over ear,
his buff eye-stripe

breaks to hear faint
thrush-spottings below
his horn-coloured eye-wattle:
as one whose weather-movements

no longer love the snow
of whitish corners, but that mournful
kind of snowfall which, close up,
seems . . . another flower.

The Mule Path

The curve of his hair across his forehead
was one long radiance from shore to shore,
giving such a bloom even to chairs and tables,
I forgot to look for the flower to be straightened
in its vase.

A string of three deaths
had woven prize seed pearls through my hair,
each like a breast sculpted in a cup,
or a ripe moon melting ivory and glass . . .

the temperature so sparklingly cool, so
in the teens, hand grenades froze
in their casings, which encircled them
dancingly, like some islands I know.

Gone were the grey, blue and black
wools, the blood-poor gardens turned black,
the looking away from people on streets,
the wind and strangled waves of the old year
made love to as a scarf.

We were living again in the year 1000,
which christened a bronze bell in an out-
of-the-way church, when the city
stepped back from itself,
and the monolingual world seemed veiled.

Everything bitter could eat the world
and its scenes of sadness leaf by leaf,
its notes left in corners: the dance-card
of my youth was his olive-wood fire,
he escorted me by boat
to his unbroken sea-air.

The Sleeping Room

This summer's evening red
is for others. Wind and light
of an earlier face
will gather the apples.

A sound, warmed by being
lived in, crumbles off
the set of the houses,
persists in being no one's.

No one has stayed underwater
longer than this hyperwakeful
need for sea or, still untouched
deep within it, Easter's voice

avoiding all my summer paths
like a round corner room
full of last June.
Day in my blood,

night in my blood,
the journey to September
lies inside me, costing me
all but your faithful hands.

The Grief Machine

I am so easily embraced, I am all taste,
a face that you like to watch.
The ice-action of my eyes, seeing through both
at once was thine own infathering.

Your upper half was mustard, suiting
the owner of my orchard, your lower was a deadly
battleship grey. In the brilliantly coloured
Last Judgement where we shall longest be,
I will feel the flat of your hands
twisting my hand in its four-buttoned
glove to your lips.

The 60s' cube and 70s' porch
of the sun-hinged church was far from locked.
It echoes your 'Amen' like a sort of reed-bed
to me, a wall of withered citrus-yellow
saints are my more than mouth-friends.

My left side blazed at the fir shadow
politeness of your kiss, pushing my shoulders'
two loops of silk into the dead,
your seed a white arc of hailstones
caught in the love-poem of my hair.

The river that threaded together
towns and cities in its current
and the fish and birds unique to it
sucked back the green of the fields
on their sides, and tightened their early
leaves into bud-like streams and valleys.

Then the prison of your tongue within
the prison of your sleep watered me

with a beautiful easy language, the language
of my clothes, story till day a night in telling,

from the bleaching moon-guest,
from the woven wood listening
in the forest-padded room
coated in the littleness of time.

The Flower of Tullahogue

1

Once again the untold Irish light,
(its nationalist purity, its everyday spite),
donated like the millennium that never came,
seems to sink slowly, to clothe itself, to swim,

as that word is understood, as if into dim
water, to keep it at brotherly length, or him
in less and less malice, while the English winters
he loved like children, grow ailing and weak and older.

2

I drove myself to Morrow Town,
a hundred towns away.
The song of the street rain
was long in never dying.

I walked there unwetted,
willing the jewelled river
to freeze stiffly facing south,
its body to form a ring.

Can it be that Spring
parading before my eyes
was warding off an epitaph
by planting something stone?

The Garryduff Bird

I was his lover of stone,
still his hand was never-resting,
an image of our boat
taking to the waters.

Through three stanzas and a song,
I learned not to tamper with his grief,
only because it comes as a touch
of kneaded wax and poured bronze

into a place found for his name
among a sequence of other names.

I had a poem dominated by time
in the ebb and flow of woodland,
a rose poem whose petal-shaped fields
are islands of cleared land

where his small, blond, romantic ghost
will bear to be written of, over and over,
after his sheerest, seeming lapse
as the just-now-quickening Christ.

The Deadest Deaths are the Best

— Montaigne

You lay, grey and quiet,
herded into a ring,
by the exploded tree,
comely as a church,
but it was I who was
nailed there firmly.

The pool through its artifice
paints Narcissus.
His arms mark
the beginning of an embrace,
an embrace that is
only a splash.

But you, my more divine
brother, you have received
a thousand times
what I yearn to have
just once: hoarfrost
to your harsher sister,

snow, that other brightness,
that slides from the world
like a river, its
ardour of self-bestowing
a flaming evidence
of wild delight, like sunlight.

The diminished promise
of your voice becomes
illegible; image and spectre,
now framed,

snake within each other.
The washed sharpsand

with supposedly gold stars
saving your name plaque from Lethe,
yet draws within me
from outside,
infinite either way,
the aisleless horizon.

My Father Walking

There are so many fathers, false fathers,
he who is only outside me is not my highest
father. But he walks ahead,
aware that he is leading someone,
as reality heads towards the light
of meaning, as what is not literature,
our lives, no more than language,
is a language that can always be spoken
by another language.

While the tide is rising, the walker
is on the island, a glaze of pious clouds
spreads over the day-close three nested cups
of tattered air, a shape which prayer
had taken. I sucked his eye
like a breast, my eye was sipped
by his lips, the act ceaselessly retraced
like the oceanic marriage of sharks
which closes over itself to caress the soul.

His fingers pressed against the thin path
of silence in my lips, his hands looking
as if they could not belong to that face,
or rested on the handle of a spade
where he bent his upper body at an angle
to the world as a rose transmits its scent
without movement. I made a despairing advance
into the décor of his life, a kind
of death ray at the purest moment of his end:

weaving seamlessly at the hour at which
people die, a kind of zero degree of the person
into my church, my worn church, a tabernacle
of words, in Latin colours, into my white-necked one.
Who gave a first voice to something before language,

water pouring with a different pulse, remorse —
his summer hair through the pages of his silence,
even when he is walking quickly.

Low Low Sunday

When I look at you hard, you seem a steady well,
fed from beneath by some dishevelled stress:
most opposite to the morning with its under-reddened face
making up for the hidden face so light in grass.

Your heart, untouched as the view, is bafflingly constant
in its heat, no more like inflamed flesh than the sunset.
Our not-quite-spoken bones are soaped clean as a lemon,
the blown clouds soak, for someone preparing to paint.

My shouldered-away kinetic blood father
is music come to an end, beyond mechanics,
body of water no longer swayed as a piece, very liquid
weather that will not remain out of doors:

aspiration upon aspiration of snow working
through the roof, trapped bubbles in a frozen pond,
blizzard of letters, ruined riverscape ferociously
on view, that rushes over a cropped opening —

my blindingly red but yesterday jet of poetry,
that fitted itself like magic into my intensive care —
is a figure of dew or grace or fire that shares
his strain of new, unreckoned time — his low Low Sunday.

Wet Birthday

Happy rain, to lie completely still,
to look out at once on two seas,
or roll the grass by moonlight.

A muscle of cloud in a four-cornered
garment, played at taking a morning
walk — my step is long in walking.

The month was a closer friend
than the day, the saddest notes of the deepening
river's voice went unanswered

by the four thousand voices which wore
their old green in the seeming-leafless
ankles of the hills. As Sunday touches

Sunday, as night and morning almost meet,
he came to me as sea air, a sculptor
where before he had been a jeweller.

The Finisher

He had some young ash trees for disposal
by the bottle shoulders of old wellsides,
a sworn man, a little in-kneed.

The year stirred like a ghost dance
through a double roof two posts ago,
in the absence of a ballad, perfectly warm.

To feign death among the dead
was the door of a room he was used to,
a summer complaint spoke to him at noon

and a robin's river action cut
a flattened musket ball
into four parts, bright as guns,

that pierced the corrupt placenames,
where the deep rose overtaken
was hanging from the ash above the well.

The Gregory Quarter-acre Clause

The fourteen-pointed star
bells out in the air
stretching across my mouth.

It is a resonantly English
over-king that has almost kissed
away my necked bowl.

Chained to me like a spoon,
my decayed thatch, it is
the island behind my island,
but not a place walked in,
creating an island effect.

Obsolete and tomb-led as
the Boyne, it sucks at my tide
as a vase food, as if the sea flowed
all around, not merely to the east.

I blush blue and exemplary
as it zips down to the river,
and flycatches the road's more
ambiguous edges, pleats the ground
with all the markers of the year
into a half-circle of older silver lamps.

After six hours, breathless as
the equator, the cropmarks rising
from their knees house
her cushion and her looking-glass,
her thimble, smock and ear-drops,
her glove and seal and Canterbury hair.

Filming the Famine

1

My meal of pleasure crisped like a wave
in the perfect circle of his lips,
not helped by the winds and the air:

the primal garment of his skin,
and the brush-braid on the hem of his voice
was an answer as soft as the question.

It was an evening made of cold clouds
and the necessary flight of natural sleep,
which takes the malice of memory into the half-world.

Springs that had carried the steely dusk
only hours old into my heart
lost their coral heartbeat and were still.

The island glittered like some silver and crimson
winter fruit. The river's small leaden blue
pulse was only sad as one is in a dream.

Its whistled lament took blood from cattle
and brought down birds — its scarlet cross-stitch
roped me into grudging prayer.

2

The image of peace was superimposed
on a sea composed of fragments,
fairground notes like a fragile line of surf
came from the stamens of her pearly fingers,
out of the shelter of her veil,
into the shadow of her arms.

She was all stranger, like some war
that had escaped out of a book,
all but Irish, fought according
to the code of the angels.

Mass paths and other useless roads
devastated by street battles,
and soldiers impersonating soldiers,
overlapped in a film presentation
of an island that had lived through
two famines, and still comes into my dreams.

Brick-makers and coal-heavers
and people without end
slid together in a cell of false time,
a summer of sorrow,
flat lines of darker black
in the sunken inkpots
of the brig *Eliza Ann,*
The Intrepid, the ship *Carrick,*
Hebron, Erin's Queen, Syrius,
Virginius, the sisters
Elizabeth and *Sarah.*

The springing forms of her hands
were a merciless screen against sight:
but if the notes were high and opened heaven —
they might suddenly hear something.

Not Yielding to the Will of Yellow

The city dilates, lying with its head
slightly downhill, as if the light of the sea
had acquired human form — there isn't
a flag but clings lank to its staff.

Stars, circles made of evergreens
show the stars, long, long before they are
due: the green which has been drawn
off begins to burn, and take the whole

window with it. My eye sweeps
led by white, to speak of blue,
the moon-forces of the moon breast
in moonlace, hanging in air.

And if the year had started
with the new moon, I should have closed
the year with death on my hand
thinking the blood out of his body,

or coaxing it out as a mere passer-
by in greyer practices. But since you
have become sound, every time a ray
of starlight touches him,

the sunlight searing itself
on to your body shines a fourfold
kiss like an inner sky of stars
far beneath his smile

to his related mouth; a world
ingredient of lived time,
with blue's quality of going away,
to accompany the blue forever.

Against Cityness

Love is a city colour,
its bloodstream is a town.
Its eyes travel the stretches of unbeing
between the too-bright lights.

One man's love is the sum
of all the routes he takes through it,
past the unconverted houses,
over the pre-city bridges,
becoming legible in the death of the streets.

Even if it is a garden city,
or a lake city,
if it is all the person is,
it is all wrong
for February to live inside your head,
as if your house were not a machine
for living in,
but constructed around a well, a lung
through which your building breathes.

I have to hunt in the most unruffled,
elegant, sedate and leafy parts
for the flavourlessness of love as twinship,
for the bruisedness of its Christian-naming talk —

an arrangement, not a fate, that spreads
its unearthly colour into nature so forecastably,
the city will float away like a wave.

The Yellowest Child

An amusing tint to the daylight
as autumn edged towards winter
split the room in two:

a love the colour of a yellowed
cameo, powdery and vanilla
on the tongue.

Father-hungry, your filial letters
left me nearly blind;
in the rocking of your arms

I missed a child who would have
come from me, not the rest
of the world.

I frequented the dying society
of your precise torments,
the mauve cast of your complexion,

your meagre human portion,
nailed to your ashen hair.
And secretly buying Masses

for one refusing care,
I unwound the russet ribbon
of your wise blue life.

Azure on a Yellow Purse

It is year three of the century.
Pastfulness has breathed its fullest:
our lilac's Persian pearl strand is still
raining a paler version to the floor.

Without time or stars the taken mountain
tapers to as long a time of darkness
as of light — windless fireflakes
pause in the matching sky.

You pick up one glint of each new wedding
and offer me with devotion only a leaf.
Your face has moved ahead of the light,
its moisture, wine on your fovea,

lets you see into the shallows of the lukewarm
angels, voyaging as far from heaven as possible:
how Nazareth, they think, once meant 'flower',
the million million ways words can die.

The Walking of the Land

Macha was not a Celtic queen but an older goddess.

— E Estyn Evans

The date was three years, three months, and three days
before my time (I shall never have a time),
but I have had the frailty of him in me.
He will want to know I am gone.

It was death that led us back through time,
inflecting the deep order with its surprise:
now he can go on further, clean as a flower,
leaving it word for word thought-true.

Because true to his own deepest need,
though it was an assisted death he dreamed
outwards, on gale days and days
of the dead, for one hour only

(it cannot be loaned). He was bedded
on winter-brown leaves with a sand-filled pillow,
where the leaf-fodder of his headstreams'
first inpouring moistened the rose-boughs

carrying sunshine in their cooling arms.
A flutter of spring-sown blood-red
forced the main stem of the thorn
through eight petals within eight petals

to the honey that never sleeps.
In a half-conquest, the 'venerable natives'
take native wives, each is drawn to the woman
by only the sail-hung half of himself;

and the ring he wears is square
with a pyramid brocaded

with a double-armed cross, like an empty
sepulchre visited by adorant youths

from which the sky-living untruth went out
to the tide-water towns, the tenders of blue
apples, the white-necked church still
curved in the shape of his sky-alone neck.

Ring Worn outside a Glove

In my mind I assigned you the place
where the rudders graze the ship,
description of your wristy demi-sleep,
turned over on its back by a breeze.

Because we do not deny the image
of a particular year, the first time
is always once again. The picture
kills the ones around its life

with ropes of useless starlight,
wasted heaven of last year's burned
palm. They shut their eyes parading
and taste themselves with the glittering

pacifism of their tongues,
as if they really were idols,
and must wither to decoration,
barbaric stone pillars we pass by.

Every proud, quietly superior word
is swept half out of the water
in the hands of your voice, that means
the thereafter shorn from their names.

Scotch Argus on Jerusalem Sage

He hutches down where grass begins
to pipe into the stem, wings locked
on the plant, the rest of him trying
to open. As termovisual a target
as all three bridges on the Danube:

the bite out of his wings by a bramble
loop, a crater on the walking path,
flight of cars in waves replaced by gestures,
he purifies the smell of burned jasmine
through his uranium pleated body.

Aged red that absorbs final sharpness,
his fine geranium coat flows from his shoulders,
videlicet lashes woven through each day,
and the jade shroud he wears beneath,
a rudder of veined protection.

He sucks the feel of the leaf from his mouth
parts, his tongue's side edges the sun's tide
across like a glowworm on a snail's back.

A green handful of fingers marks his increasing
white, twin wing eye-spots lank against
the offering air.

The Palace of Today

The meaning is very much
a rhythmical one, the same law
in blossom on the shoulder-high
fork of a shrub-like tree,
just streaming out presence
and expecting nothing.

The pew resembles a half-open
tomb or a sort of kennel
for gazing out of themselves,
their lives overgrown like an old path,
turning into their opposite,
when they let the handkerchief fall.

The slowness of his tread
seems to call for no great effort,
it revolves only thirty times a minute.
Because the treads are set so
very far apart, he has to stretch
his limbs to their utmost

in order to reach the step,
so that one of his legs is always
in mid-air, and takes the whole
of his weight when it lands.
During this his body remains
completely motionless,

the slowness of the movement
is enough to make his head spin
and strain the muscles of his stomach.
Sometimes he loses consciousness
and falls from the top of the wheel.
I watched men and children

as they came off, and not one
had the slightest trace of sweat,
on the contrary, all appeared
to be cold, all pale, almost blue,
like the sage-brush branch our carriage
caught, near steps of unpeeled log.

To My Disordered Muse

The wall itself was almost hidden in summer
once the glens were opened, the commonness between us.
But there comes a time in life when the senses
change places, or the brain takes all that the seasons
describe, and cannot wait for the first snowfall.

The divisions of the town passed through his own
body, existing without, and without, and without,
the several cities in one, the bell-tongues and blood-
greased stones, the garden of masts, ships which fill
every inch of the tartan river, its last seaward turn.

As if his scentful heart is squeezed in a vice,
the more it is trodden, the more it will spread,
and its energies bleed a ring of seeds,
I dream that he treads on a lily, and dreams of
geraniums, or larch that grows six times faster than oak.

Light, daylight-white, placed over water
structures the water — looking at the ruby-red
shining of the colour on his body, he didn't
so much as move his eyes one-fortieth
the brightness of a sunny day.

His irises not quite touching the lower lids,
as when we tell our day, or a few of the day's
waves. A moment's pause that soldiers know,
his summer-led body slipped into the morning,
and drums were swiftly stripped of their muffling crêpe.

His chest on the cross-bar, his belted thighs and ankles,
the leader trimming the tails through his left fist
to soften the leather with his saline sweat,
removing the thick blood that would cushion
the blows, placing the patterns where they wished,

each numbered stroke accompanied by drum-roll
and tap, till the lash fell with the lightness
of a feather, jerking his head, and the hands
and feet of the watchers turned cold
from sucking in the tears if they wept.

It may require a knife-blade, or the wisest
cloud of all in the chiming sky,
to change universe verbally, in a tided town,
and achieve a waking in an hourless house
entered by no road, by a body not your own.

The Muse-hater's Small Green Passion

Since that trim February,
enough connected days
went aloud in a letter
a long way round
to awaken your nightside image

as centuries take a while
to disappear,
as a blessed century
smooths out in a matching fabric
after the march of words
and corridors of how long.

A differentness has begun
like the growth of grass, hair-thin
in spear-feet, the sword-lily
after the lack of irises.

More slowly than the eye passes,
leaving us with too much
for the journey, the square miles
of suffering shape the bed,
the house, the book, into
the laziness applied to fields.

So we can travel across ourselves
in tidy months
mobile as a language
from the well-knownness
of your lighted parts
and lightless state of mind

even on the jade of Death
with goblet and bridle,
to the well-marked bone

at the root of your breast
that promised to be a woman;

to the hinged opening
and secluded swannery
of the wood-carved, never-
satisfied manliness
of your inner wall.

Even in tragedy, they were such risks
to my deadness, the angel ceasing
to be an angel, this sharpness
and stretch of pure profile wings
like a downpour of stars.

Clara Theme

There is no Muse outside the soul.

— Hölderlin

It seems un-Christmassy,
a non-singing robin
fasting in a tree-cavity
with its neck drawn in.

His beard has been wound around
with gold thread,
his lungs like the lungs of the sea,
black and set.

An abortive melody
stopped at a moment of its growth,
silk mosquito nets
sailing him into the sea's lap
at horse-flesh speed.

He had just discovered,
looking at snow-clad fields
in the sun, how to paint
impalpable white trees of spring

when the edges of the world
became dark before his eyes,
going blind after a walk in the rain;

and his tongue felt lame
as if he had stripped off
his body too soon —

the bird-listener,
picturing his birdsong,
heard the slate-tinged yellow
rhyming with the velvety
lightness of the table

with its trinity of fruit
when he came into song,
like quickborn glass
speckled with gold,

a building bird
suspending woven pouches
from the tips of branches.

∾

When such a rock speaks,
the breadth of a road
beaten by travellers
pulls the iron out of it

to carry one fall
of his almost spectral hair —
a rough altar, for this collared prey
of a songster.

Black Magnificat

for Neil Jordan and Patrick McCabe

Our voices mild and moist,
baptized with dark water.
The mobile stroking hand
soaking my shoulder.

A rain-affected
smooth execution,
sure to be too light,
a mere film,

forcing out the real name
of the hardest-worked river
beyond the bounds of the city
and the neglected old fields.

I cup one hand over my eyes
stiff with many inner deaths,
and in a crush of images
with a kissing sound at the ear

appears the moon like a beheading
block, its moon volume
only half-born, a surliness
beating in and between

like a jealousy or soreness
whose warmth never closes —
opened, but not broken open.
You flower her, create

new spotless local inhabitants
for this harrowed moon
whose power hovers on a ribbon,
but it will not be the same Paradise.

His Minstrelization

Dilation of spirit: his face is almost condensed.
His hands act as guards to the eyes'
sideview of heaven, or clasp his skull,
veins raised spectacularly where the turned head
touches the nude neck.

Even if one gave up sleep entirely,
we cannot know where he looks
with that double-souled, pushing look,
at a space scooped out or blown clear
in one act of vision,

his windswept interiors
allowed to stain a range of rusts
directly, or in all directions,
as that jagged spray of cedar
issues from the entireness of the plant.

The river so magical above
the repeated arms;
the folded blanket, stale,
when a milder eye was in fact available,
just then finding its postwar shape.

The Pyx Sleeper

Now where sensuousness begins
the air enjoys him, his open-air heart,
his open-eyed dream, his sexless sex.

What he is to me is to me
all that he is, he is for me
what he alone can ever be for me.

I delight without envy in his form,
his imparted self, the hidden and assured
oxygen and salt of my existence.

The new and ever newer water,
not the sterile baptismal water,
is the image of his eye, his natural mirror.

But why does his reflection
already want to wound me?
I know that he will still be the one

who someday takes my inward broken life,
but neither would I wish
that my soul be scattered.

There is nothing that makes passion
less transparent than the passionless
light, its miracles of anger,

receiving the rejected nature
into his heart again. We have a world
between us, exactly a world, and the nothing

out of which the world came
is nothing without the world.
I take hold of the purely thinkable

body with my lips closed, unclosed,
as if there were a rune less divine
that could make him mine.

The Chamomile Lawn

My body cannot forget your body,
the day is only blanched in the open spaces.
White gardens grow up through the fixed scent
of earlier roses, that give the impression
of being undiscovered solid roses.
In moments of such nearness,
heaven lies close upon the earth, lends seed
along the length of the bed; life is held
only from the tip of the lips, you close
your eyes to keep life out, and breathe

into the heart upon paper, the area that hurts.

A view of the street, with the world
as background, shows people dashed about
as by a terrible wind of death — Death week,
its distinct seasonal corners. I hear my death speak,
making silencing gestures while he speaks
through all the other deaths in the room,
as if the tree-wasting coffins could recognise
the decay around them and be each other's death.
Though this is a town governed by its flowers,
the dyes have been fixed for twenty years.

I had never troubled to go that short journey,
into a land of unmetalled roads,
where snow lay till it melted
and was simply weather, a second coat
a layer of silence on the cultivable ground:
like a river-mouth without any river,
or what a man does when he ceases
to be violent, to injure his outer self,
and nothing else moves in him
but the very last extreme of fear,
he empties his revolver into the mirror.

With an air of vine-leaves about his brow,
but wounded in his wish, he need not
guard against death anymore. My head
and heart line up behind him, my legs' darkness
fold around his waist. He pours his blood out
striving to free his *I* from the *I*,
and finds himself to be so non-masterfully
that indescribably delicate personality
of light by which he sees, this quartered
death is worth a whole life, my life, me.

Corduroy Road

That now historical ground
of growing wheat, an oatfield,
a clover field, not far from Richmond,

is faded into light green,
ripe and suffering,
is covered with dirt and pitch,
the sentimentalized blossoms
outlast the stench.

This is the day that went unmolested,
a Mass fast day, a time for reverence
to flags, even to the year-long never flags.

They are doing penance for it,
kneeling on all fours, tables
in the east of our houses.

I have called them woods but they
were nothing, one horse captains,
out of the woods-world behind us.

It was a compass built into me,
the militarization of my thought,
their shots were to me like voices;

I would go outside and lie
naked in the dry sand
for their Caravat lips, because they were
dry and folded, for their Hassidic sidecurls.

I have just counted
the wind of giddy bullets
woven into my bread.

That minute dies
without opening his head,
and yet he lived a little while,
he is sleeping in a garden close by here.

Others were spirited away
to black freedom,
plunging into the unburying earth
of the desired Ireland,

young, precious, ferocious, fresh death,
death of the day, today's death . . .

but there's breath, let's keep it,
till it's what we are made of.

Upper Nazareth

His was a particularly
wasteful death —
like glass or cactus
in your throats,
to non-expert eyes
such as mine.

When the main thing missing
was a country,
his naming and renaming
of the place
brought the unpromising marshland
to virility,

and the dolorous country
a comprehensive peace,
with names like 'Crazy'
or 'Tomorrow'.

He turned old fields
into new ones,
and the amorphous field,
essentially empty and patient,
into the habitual Atlantic.

His shell-game,
not one sound but every sound,
was the almost casual prayer
for everything to the east
of an imaginary line,

for fields left unprayed for
at the sovereign point,
and mostly frozen.

Pincushion with Beaded Cross

Today, an air day, I fear
the horizon of the city —
an image worth dying for,
though some people lived
so poetically there . . .

and though I belong so little
to the more present present,
nine years' worth of real silences
lay unheralded
like letters clustered about a date
in a deeper layer of truth.

The blue overran, one pale-blue
cobalt sheet folded into quarters
I made my same-day, even one more
letter, my thirty-ninth,
now nameable,

to the friend whose name
does not matter: the one who thinks
music is his own account
of what it is like to be him.
I have been so plagued by music

today, tell me, without music,
through some honest person as an angel,
where the ordinary, not special, dead
slip to, best seen with closed eyes,
when they no longer dream themselves,

but you dream for them;
and, long asleep in Christ,
both push them away

to forget them so completely,
and wake them alive

suspiciously long,
till prayers *for* change
to sacred prayers *to*. Thank you a moment
for what you do and do not tell
me, dying traveller,

wave-scrolled with the moon's help,
by the same turnings and same trees,
a choir of muses pronouncing your name
for its name, miracle leading to
more miracle, and hours which do not flow.

Locust in the Cemetery

The grave was my favoured post-box,
as difficult as a flower. There was no give
in the fabric of its one-piece floor, walls
and roof, but I slipped into its black
accent, using his photograph as a fan
which gave the dark a pedigree of cinnamon
lashes. My kiss on wood that hollowed
to receive it was a whisper in the hush
reflected off the folded blue roses
bigger than his fist which formed
a silver necklace in the centre, like women
I'd heard laughing while I was growing up.

I laid my body across his
in the shape of a cross, I cut myself
a grave across his head: I took
a meal at the grave by setting
two vases mouth to mouth in his
Gioconda smile, and then I burned
his body in its tomb and drowned
the burnt bones in honey in a gold
dish — so when he kisses the drinker
of this terrifying peace, oblivion
which is not to be hired
will be his slave.

The Sleep Cure

The sea is the act of wiping,
a thought unhesitatingly
pointing into a sign.
A loving mouth bursts through it
like a natural gate.

When death floods a rasping
sweetness into the room,
you always feel yourself
to be much stronger,
you lock up the sea

far from your own life
in the mocking indoors of dreams
whose silence you have basely,
coarsely reached for,
whose neck you could wring.

Persons or streets
who give nothing but themselves
imitate the nothingness
of a bed that overtakes
each movement that our body sketches out

and vanishes spring-smelling
behind a wooden screen
till all that is left
of even the scent of melancholy
is the sky counting

in different sheets
of mauve transparent paper,
with my inward April
a number within it
alone with the boatman.

The Self-concealing

Now, now, words for it,
the eyelids of those eyes,
the eyes' blue school,
whose school is the school of heaven.

To where could we step back
from this destiny of denial
whose fourfoldedness
encircles the globe?

Not only through a ringing out
of its voices,
but with the greatest difficulty
can we hear the silent voice

of this joining. The name flows
from the naming,
and more willingly
beauty dwells on earth, but spares

its appearing, as its ownmost self.
The earth replies by its own
movement, the ray of light
that meets the newborn,

with the old saying of their togetherness.
Insofar as death comes, it vanishes,
and whether it comes from afar,
it is also a life.

Gander Month

The years that are over
govern his loneliness,
his final berth
made a high sky.

I want you, frail,
careful people,
gun-conscious, gun-polishing,
gun-displaying,

to understand me wrong:
and the poetry into which
my burned heart
would go for you

to be remembered
only by heart.
I didn't go forward
to the touch

of the rotted rose-leaves
cupped among
descending pines,
but how much

my thinking was entangled
in the white jade
of his eyelashes,
the emerald facings

on his dinner jacket,
the slow pull and push
of his deer-rifle
turning the whole temple blue.

The Scissors Collection

Red house, red week, red springtime:
card-carrying freshness hoarded from childhood.
Though we did not reach the empire of signs
I overheard in your child-verb-city
all the earth's principal languages
spoken in hushed voices — spoken in torrential
but everyday voices, by the gracious,
distant, antiquated silhouette
of the fir trees, unreeling miles and miles
of voice powerful enough to kill moonlight.

Timbered porches, balconies hanging over
empty space stole our instincts. Our poetry
boutique was a sort of pastry palace on two levels
reined in by a double sweep of stairs.
Its rooms were not designed, with their pointed,
clover-leaf windows, to be lived in by day.
Like a living creature entered
in a coat of arms, old Europe
couldn't raise a cup to our lips, but held
our eyes on overturned chairs for a swallowed time.

I was appeased by the endless, oversized
sky, that felt like part of the morning,
or nature where there is no nature, wearing
a cavalry badge on her gold bracelet.
Ave Maria time altered the lighting
on your past; it wrapped our shoes in felt
like mountains walled into their own happiness.
Stone flames arose from pots, a granite piano
decorated a composer's grave, we suffered
through one Mozart, two Schuberts and four Liszts.

Though they have music built into their names,
their spirit of havoc, vital, reassuring disorder,

we were ill-assorted, semi-experiences,
my porcelain washbasin with slate blue flowers
wept all the tears in my body. I covered
the lamp on my night-table with a handkerchief,
like a small, irregular breast. Your father
buried in his red Garibaldian shirt
suddenly kissed my black-clad father's
worker's hands for ten minutes.

Palm's breadth of green water. So beautiful
when it is beautiful. The wild new life
of a blond-wood desk felling something sure
in a Bible paper word. Even if a brother died
the day a bird was brought home, embellishing
your signature with another sharp, we are
only responsible for our lives starting
on a particular day. An unusually long-held
wavering first-hand shot blurs the kind
of incandescent, long hair that you love.

Crystal Night

Our friends, the enemy,
gambled away eternity
for ten years of wasteland,
a spout of soil where field
was laid unto field
below a street as wide
as the height of the houses.

For seven days yearly,
a murder timed to coincide
with the summer solstice,
they parade their boots, drums, songs,
their undinist rhythms, insignia, flags,
their uniforms and pageantry,
their forests of banners,

their declarations of loyalty,
their endless repetitions of slogans,
their standard greetings,
their catechetical speeches,
their myopic, frustrated
ideology of the cheated
through the city of convulsionaries.

Prizing words only as fists,
or a series of insipid rosettes
that stand for protest,
at the chaste hour,
to appease the major-domos,
the ballet-masters danced
their choirs as if their columns
could conquer space.

As the earth is moved
from its position

by the weight of even a tiny bird
resting upon it,
so each gun, moved into position
by nine tractors, required a crane
to insert each shell.

They would shoot high
if we would rearrange the earth
like the dust when a table
is struck. They would take care
to make their arms so encircling,
pious and elegant
as melted-down church bells

for a cannon to comb
a spider's web with its nailed
tongue, tearing his gliding
spinal cord from the cover
of his limbs,
that can never be bent
backwards or forwards.

And among all these injured things,
when the dwellers emerged slowly
to meet their liberators,
like a belated crowd
lost on a cricket pitch,
the goldfinch, its breast filled with lilies,
carried, torch-downward, the spurge.

Pilgrimage to Poland

Oh lean kine! Your unribbed blue,
arme blanche, *bête noire*,
black rose in the new dyes
of my mind!

When the ovaries are resting
their half-silvered bulbs,
to be anywhere but Ireland
is usefully to be called English:

centuries of enforced openness
and sawing up bunks to make room
for rifles — vaseline and straw
everywhere — was my late being.

The wild and mere Irish rivers
were among the wedding-guests,
your English-Irished sweethearts,
weaving the king's peace.

I who had felt obliged
to climb the stairs of Irish history
found there your bright cuirass
of a country and your black wing

of hair clearing the rubbish
from the mouth of the Sybil's cave,
as a young man collects
blossoms to his face.

When they lower the white flag,
then drop it, one death
comes lower and lower,
then touches the ground,

depleting the world of life
like a drying harbour.
So an arm shepherding the air
like a cavalry sabre

on a more comprehending
day of creation
snowed an occult, aromal rose
in a portal ceremony

between an abyss and a hawk —
a florid coin, a fit house,
a meet bed, and an apt cloak
to cheer those inly mourned.

Jeszcze Polska

in memory of Dawid Sierakowiak

Do not behave like prey
if I feather-touch or almost touch
the long, heavy sea-shell
of your Davidstern.

> My hands begin to burn
> at how very softly it is possible
> to touch someone.

A slow-eyed kiss
is thrown from afar,
a mouth-hug fitted
to your war.

> Shine appearing
> diagonally across your tongue,
> your pinch-pleated cheek-pouch.

And half-a-glass
of my blood
from lips to lips
down the centre of your throat —

> snow crumbs
> on the weather-edge
> of your unleashed spirit,

something living, something
still alive, a more human sun
than the blissful sound of bombs
through your days of first-class hunger.

                                        Twelve planes in triangles
                                        of three, steel-green,
                                        form a letter whose meaning
                                        nobody knows

like large mourning candlesticks
white as snow-uniforms
around the Jewish-yellow
of your gun-hand swing loosely.

                                        Is it the newspapers
                                        that have died
                                        without the least rustle?

As though I divide
every bearable passing day
when July begins like this
with fields made slippery by mist,

                                        some of your Augustan calm
                                        is what I am trying to send
                                        this cleaner spring: your
                                            Marne,
                                        oh, Marne! . . . please happen
                                            again.

On the Mulberry Tree at Heilsbrück

Voices on propped elbows
go warmly through the air;
tongues lift, and yet
do not lift, in the fledgling
current of the oblong room,

an arch of living green
where a deformed tree bulks,
its corrugations so smooth,
it seems a crossed leg
moulded in bothsex pewter.

A vine's still timid fire
thick as overhead dew,
hot as my sweat that dropped
in the dust, lends the blue taste
that the clouds like best

to the sky's rebellion
opening behind me.
A mouthful of us,
and what was already burnt
is now our bidden friend,

the heather roots burning away
so deep underground,
your cross-sea heart
beats from an outer court
to an inner hour of road

when the other goods train
moves out first:
denying pasture, undoing
on one naked side
the detail of the nipple

on the breast attacked
and emptied every inch,
like that ungleaming petal, Honesty,
that starts in fullest blood,
then marbles to an outshone bud.

A Deserted Landing-stage on the Rhine

Minute by minute throughout
those fourteen hours and ten minutes,
I remembered again your water's
beating yellow dimness,

your flowing hill-line,
the humid stinging scent
of any one field browning out
Germany's harvest quality.

Now that at least four names
crowd on to me, with an air
of having lost everything, the old
unity, of the great-hearted,

patient and understanding city,
whose rivers showed up black,
where the phosphorescence of rotten wood
absorbed with a purring sound

that year's angels, I see how you enter
into a love of the roofless half
of Bonn, Europe's museum
dripping with peace; so we swam

in peace, and no one knew
what to do with all that peace;
and everyone was poor, and no one
was smart, and there was no sin,

while the known dead lay like
a dawn of leaves in the access streets,
astonishing the night by thinking
day. It has been blown away

as we explained ourselves under
What We Have Been Through, or discussing
love in music — your Apollonian Rhine
with its destroyed bridges over it

as though it were unfolded from my own flesh.

Pale Adjective

Like a window in a throne
her ring contained a scent,
a momentary furrow
of jade veined salt-white.

The future had broken in
so powerfully that blind men
were led to the place,
feast-scene of a funeral by moonlight.

To sell a dream that follows the mouth
and is taken in by nets,
the city has the ocean
for a pavement.

Since on dying we are roused
and interrogated,
and at the moment of being born
there is no horizon.

Forcing Music to Speak

And the napkin, which was about his head, not lying with the linen cloths, but rolled up in a place by itself.

— John 20

for Eamonn Whelan

I love a church of lanterns
and narrative windows,
the light of old churches . . .

the shell of the bride of Christ
stains a universe whose gravity
is too weak to wrap its space around

until it joins up with itself,
using the patterns of goddesses
to carve with snow-knives a rain animal,

a lily of the valley, not
of the heights. Much to my awakening,
the illness spirits come close,

but I have no ear for their whispering:
the essence of their ghostliness,
shapes ten miles in time

that fail to reach eternal life
and have to buy each day.
To the east, a young man,

like a doll pruned from a live tree,
a female birch, standing on the corner
of a wall of the building,

thanks Radegund for her gift of chestnuts,
admires the graceful, sculpted cut
of Agnes' fingers, of which he finds a print

in the butter rising to the top of the milk
she sent him. Tree of music.
Like grass when greenness flows into it.

Greenest stem scenting all dry spices,
standing leafy in his nobility
as dawn breaks, his feet glowing like the dawn

through her secret, among the living rafters.
We cannot see his eyes, and can discern
only a hint of his mouth,

but this is where he stood,
his signature included,
delivering his body, his whirling,

musical body, musical glove, to the music
he knew in the sky.
A harp adorned with strings lies across his body,

in his chest, and answers to every touch.
A white cloud by his mouth,
he stands on a platform left by ruins

from the eighteenth century,
before diving into the early nineteenth:
a moment in which his head

is cast in shadow and his lower body melts,
his face bowed suspended,
though his inner strength beats from his heart

like a face. He has flung himself
as from a pier, featherweight,
vertical, post-human, resonant,

he is without a body,
broken in two by his fall,
paraded to the real places

free of all body, his breath
giving out before his song.
His lifeblood

a scarlet flood of sound
with something dark and thirsty about it,
it perishes much too soon,

and states this lack clearly,
the brilliance of the voice
altogether used up.

A shock wounds his windpipe,
one is too dark, the other splits his throat,
liable to rend from within.

But at the smallest particles of dust
his slit throat resounds,
like womb-wheat or a guitar of God,

his severed head continues to sing
as it floats down the Heber
and is immersed in stagnant winter water

to land on the island of Lesbos.
Winnowed and purged and stellified —
true forge embroidered in gold and writing —

I don't want,
I don't want you
to rest in the leisure times of the cosmos:

for we do not sing 'Requiem'
for such a soul,
but the 'Gaudeamus' Mass.

His burial place, like the burial place of the great French orator, Miribeau [sic], remains unknown. His enemies seemed to have wished that his dust might mingle with the earth obscurely; that no pilgrimages might come to his tomb and keep living the cause he served. And by so doing they have unwillingly made all Ireland his tomb.

— W B Yeats
New York, 1904